12 Minutes

The Untold Story of the Ghost Plane at The Battle of the Bulge

RALPH COLEMAN GRAHAM

ISBN 978-1-0980-4491-6 (paperback)
ISBN 978-1-0980-4492-3 (hardcover)
ISBN 978-1-0980-4493-0 (digital)

Christian Faith Publishing, Inc.
832 Park Avenue
Meadville, PA 16335
www.christianfaithpublishing.com

Printed in the United States of America

For my mom and dad, for the work
you did and the life you lived

PREFACE

This book was written by a veteran of World War II, who at the age of eighteen volunteered his services fourteen months before the beginning of the attack at Pearl Harbor and the Declaration of War.

For sixteen months, he served in the regular army with the Engineer Corps before transferring to the Air Corps. Although his combat service was with the 8th Air Force in Europe, he reveals some very interesting stories about our prewar depressed years. He was a part of the 487th Bombarbment Group.

The main story line of the book concerns the year he spent in combat, the missions he flew, including the final engagement known as The Belgium Bulge, and finally to the finishing of his career at the end of the war in Europe. In the end, he reveals some of the most interesting and, in some cases, the most unbelievable experiences of the war.

Ralph Coleman Graham
Radio operator, patriot, and author
"At peace with his memories"

CHAPTER 1

Birth of This Book

Ever since I left the service some seventy years ago, I have wanted to write the story of that epic mission flown on December 24, 1944. From time to time, I would write of that day so I would never forget what occurred.

As the only living survivor of our crew, I feel deeply obligated to tell our story in order to correct not only the losses and mistakes made and never corrected but also the accounts of that event which were overlooked.

I realize there will be some who will challenge the mind and the sanity of a man who served that long ago knowing he has to be in his midnineties, and they are right in such a challenge. All I can say is I've been so lucky and blessed that my health has never been an issue.

The story of that epic mission is written by me, the radio operator of the ghost plane that was supposedly lost in the air battle but was never involved in the attack. We unashamedly discussed it back then that somewhere among the celestial landscape there was a guiding hand that led a bunch of kids through that valley of the unknown. Several times, our crew would gather at various locations and talk of the past and how fortunate we were.

Finally, at the last of our reunions, there were only three of us left. Today, as I attempt to finish this account of one of the most important combat encounters, I, the writer, am the only remaining crewmember. They would have been pleased I am setting the record straight.

This is my true story which covers graduating from high school in the year 1940, ending my first job as a farm worker picking cotton in West Texas to join the regular army, serving sixteen months in the Engineer Battalion and then transferring to the Army Air Corps. After training at several points throughout the states, I was deployed to the European theater to serve with the Army Air Corps as a radio operator with the 8th Air Force. I completed thirty-three missions of high altitude bombing in a B-17 bomber over Europe.

After a lot of years had passed and numerous discussions among our crew when we would gather for reunions, all of us agreed that what we knew happened on some of our missions were recorded incorrectly. The main story we felt needed correcting happened on the mission of December 24, 1944, during The Battle of the Bulge. It is included in the book.

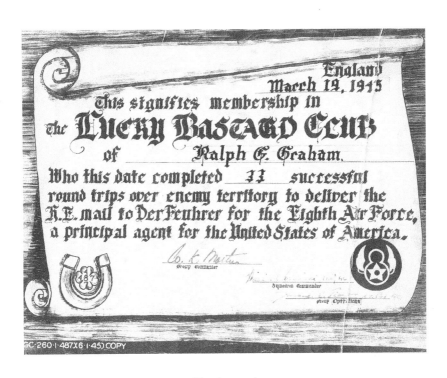

England
March 19, 1945
This signifies membership in
the **Lucky Bastard Club**
of _____ Ralph E. Graham.
Who this date completed _____ 33 _____ successful round trips over enemy territory to deliver the R.E. mail to Der Feuhrer for the Eighth Air Force, a principal agent for the United States of America.

Group Commander

Squadron Commander

Group Operations

GC-260-1-487X6-1-45) COPY

Final award

CHAPTER 2

Depression

The year was 1940. Early summer was upon us. High school graduation was over, and here I am, a highly educated young man with a gold class ring and a new sheepskin diploma to prove it. I took my personal inventory, and to my not very shocking surprise, that was it. Well anyway, knowing that there were lots of new worlds out there to conquer, I headed to my new job picking cotton in Rule, Texas.

After an uneventful trip in the back on a new flatbed truck, my friend and cousin, Dugger, and I surveyed the vast fields of white farmland and an old run-down ranch house that was to be our home while our job lasted.

After a couple of days in the field and six meals of hoecakes and dried beans, we realized this was not what the future sounded like at our graduation speeches. So we pulled up stakes, made our peace with our friends and family, and headed for what was to be our new job—the US Army.

We left early on our new adventure by the way of hitchhiking. I remember passing that last row of cotton, I pulled a green bole and said to Dugger, "Hey, this is the last bole of cotton I ever intend to pick," and threw it high into the air. I think maybe forty years ago, I did pull a bole to see if it would wink at me. It didn't.

On our first ride, we asked the fellow how far he was going, and he said Fort Worth. Good, we said, we would ride with him. What luck we caught two more rides and were home by two o'clock that afternoon.

I knew we were lucky. The folks with whom we rode were so nice that they even offered us money. Perhaps that kindness led us to realize how fortunate we were to have such a wonderful home and family. They had done so much to bring us this far.

Let me explain, Dugger and I had grown up together and became almost like brothers. We lived a short distance apart, and we worked, played, hunted, and attended school together. So it was natural for us to want to join the army together.

After we arrived back home, we began to make arrangements to go to the nearest recruiting office. Among other things, we had to seek permission from our parents to leave for the army.

When I was told that Dugger could not go because of his health, I was saddened to no end. We had been together since childhood, and I was sad to end our close relationship. I knew that we would never again be like we were as kids growing up. We had always hunted together, and we worked together in the fields. Our parents had let us learn to plow together even at age nine. They would let us plow middles between the rows of our crops. There were a lot of fond memories I had to set aside as I was leaving to serve our country.

As I write this, I hesitate now and then to check some of the facts. Then comes the stark realization that there is no one left and no records except for one person's memory.

Before I begin, I must say that the happiest time of my life was spent in these short years. As a family, we lived, we worked, we struggled, and we would laugh and sometimes weep. But in the end, we rejoiced together, and I know my life was grounded in faith and hope due to the way I was raised.

Just to give you some idea of how the works of a parent can be remembered, I can tell you as a young boy, I saw my father walk two miles to a public highway to hitch a ride to the county seat to pay his poll tax. Yes, in those days, you paid to vote. I remember watching the family wagon travel along a paved road, listening to the newly shoed horses clicking their new shoes on the pavement as they pulled us to church.

It's those wondrously innocent moments of our times that stitch together to become then and now the glue that holds our community together.

When I was a three-year-old child in 1925, my father bought a farm. This might shake you up! He bought 126 acres for $1,100 financed over forty years—the payments were $12 every six months. I do remember when he made his last payment after WWII had ended.

You know, to be able to remember all of this from start to finish has been a mystery in itself. The joy of being able to pen these little accounts of some of the things I remember has truly been a grant from above.

In order that the accounts of which I write do not become boring, most will contain some historical events of that time period of which you may or may not have been aware.

The depression brought many changes, to small communities, towns, and counties as well as the federal government. Because of overproduction, one of the most heartbreaking and memorable events was watching cattle being slaughtered, pulled away, and burned or buried. As a thirteen-year-old, it was sad to watch the cattle fall before you could hear the report from the rifle. Beautiful beef cattle that no one was allowed to consume, farmers' cotton acreage being allotted, overplanted fields being plowed under so overproducing would not occur again.

It was during this era, the darkest period of the depression, that a glimmer of hope appeared on the horizon, when the oil industry began leasing land with mineral rights and started drilling.

Not many are left that remember the old wooden derricks that puffed steam and smoke you could smell for miles away. These were the early days when there were no blowout preventers, so they would drill until oil would blow out through the derrick and sometimes catch fire. Then all the nearby landowners would think everyone would become rich. Kids would dream of new bikes and red wagons and trips to the state fair. In most cases, it became only a dream.

I want to end this depression story of how it was, but I want to tell one more. It was truly a lapse of thought and preparation by our school system. A new school was built, but someone failed to check the water system. It tasted so bad you couldn't drink it even when thirsty. Us kids would take off during recess and lunchtime and go to our neighbors well. We were warned but never punished.

A final story concerning the youth of that time. A new highway ran through our county, hiring kids from ten to fifteen years old to set out sprigs of grass on the slopes of the new construction for $1 a day. They started at sunup, yours truly included, and worked until lunch. Then we started again and worked until sundown. After that, we would run and fight all the way to the swimming pool and swim until someone came for us. Even as I pen this now, I grit my teeth with tears in my eyes as I remember that youthful Greatest Generation that did such a wonderful job in bringing peace to the world again.

CHAPTER 3

Enlist in the US Army

Only a few days passed until all arrangements were made for us to take our oath to serve our country. We were to serve one year, and that would fulfill our military obligation. Until we were called, I wanted to spend some time, kind of reliving my life and remembering how it was during those depressed years tying up loose ends and expressing my feelings with Mom. I knew this short time would probably be my last to be at home.

Now it was time to say goodbye to Mom and leave home for the last time to finish our requirements. Next, we were to have a complete physical and be sworn in at Tyler, Texas. Now, we belonged to Uncle Sam. First, they fed us and then put us on a Greyhound bus to San Antonio. We arrived in the early morning at Dodd Field, which was a boot camp and tent city outside of Fort Sam Houston. We were assigned to a big pot-bellied drill sergeant, one of the meanest but one of the best. We learned to both hate him and love him, although he had trouble spelling his own name. He was a joy to be around. He taught us much about army life and how to become soldiers.

While in boot camp, we learned quite a lot about the old army from our drill sergeant. He explained why he made the army his career. Among the many advantages he talked about were how they were well fed and well clothed, for instance, the prewar dress code required issuing creased shirts with epaulets. You were issued regular army boots, and for off duty, you were issued Garrison shoes made of highly finished leather. The overcoats personally fastened with brass buttons and belt buckles. Before the big expansion for the war, they wore leggings and campaign hats, the kind that was fastened underneath the chin with acorn buttons.

Other features that made the old army so attractive were special work programs. One, for instance, was called "Detached Enlisted Men's List (DEML)." We called it "Don't Ever Mention Labor." Let me explain. If let's say the infantry battalion needed carpentry work done which the engineers were trained to do, the men would temporally be transferred there, as DEML, until the work was finished. They were then returned back to their units. The same thing occurred with other units that needed personal skills. It did save a lot of money that way.

The interesting but dreadful memory of tent city was that 1800 men were poisoned at breakfast one early morning. Contaminated powdered eggs caused it. I still remember so well that Billy Hall, my best buddy, and I made breakfast of Post Toasties and bottled milk. We were very lucky as we watched hundreds vomiting on every corner as they waited for ambulances on every street to carry them to Fort Sam Hospital.

Several weeks passed until we finished boot camp, and then we were transferred to Fort Sam Houston and assigned to the 2nd Engineer Battalion.

At the time we entered the service in 1940, it was obvious to even new recruits the bad shape of our economy. Our military equipment was run down, almost equal to the rest of our depressed economy. For instance, our entire battalion—four companies plus three motor pools—had only one Diamond T winch truck, and it would not pull itself out of a mud hole even unloaded. Can you imagine a battalion of more than seven hundred men being commanded by a west point officer with the rank of major?

Let me tell you what we did have that was top notch—a proud infantry division that prided itself in its' every phase of operation. I'll give you an example: a battalion of engineers set a record that probably still stands. They constructed a 200 ft. pontoon bridge across an inlet of the wood lawn lake in forty-four minutes! Such was the quality of the old Indian Head 2nd Infantry Division, our infantry division. I suppose it is still deployed to South Korea, where it has been since the end of WWII.

They say always tell it like it is. This concerns a young nineteen-year-old motorcyclist that we called Robby. Another reminder of how thin our equipment inventory was at our company motor pools was we had only one motorcyclist, and yes, it was Robby. The problem was Robby could not stay out of the brig. It was amazing, indeed, to watch him direct the convoy down a public highway, through small towns, through red lights, and through intersections. I can hear him now as he roared past the convoy of trucks and equipment slinging gravel against the trucks and cars, then seeing him as he is directing traffic as we passed. Once, our battalion was chosen to lead the whole infantry division across half of Texas into Louisiana to participate in maneuvers (battle games). I can hear our battalion commander now. "We have some new cyclists, but I'll not attempt this trip without him. Go get Robby. If he is in jail, tell them to pin his Sgt. Stripes on with a safety pin and let's move."

A lot of time has passed since those dark days of the early 1940s, and I sometimes wonder if I'm the only ex-member of the 2nd Infantry Division that served there with then Colonel Eisenhower. Let me explain why. When I entered the service in late 1940, I was the youngest member of my company unit of 170 men. I was eighteen years old. This was a picture of the regular army some thirteen months before Pearl Harbor. Colonel Eisenhower, who wore a Silver Eagle on his uniform, no one really knew his real rank except maybe General George C. Marshal and others, for he was hidden in rank. The whole world soon found out who he was shortly after the war began. Eisenhower was kept hidden in the ranks as a colonel so as to not allow the Germans to know whom they would have to deal with. He was a four-star general who would become a five-star general as supreme commander of the Allied Forces. Even though my time with the division ended soon after the war began, the training and maturity I received while there proved invaluable time after time during my combat experience.

One of my most valuable training experiences came during an exercise to make men out of boys. It began on an early sunny morning. We began a march that lasted all day and night. We would have breaks every so often when it seemed we could go no farther. The night began with a slight mist that would turn into rain and finally a thunderstorm. I vividly recall times when we would halt to take a break; you would drop to the ground with your head on your pack and fall asleep with rain hitting your face. Then we were up again and would continue the march until day began to break. There was a long tree line hill. We were to attack a machine gun nests along its ridge. They showed us how to attack a machine gun nest with three men. Two riflemen would cover one man as he advanced and then switch, and again the machine gunner could not fire without exposing himself until he was forced to surrender. As the sun began to rise, the motor pool rolled up to carry us back to camp. What a relief and what an accomplishment. The tough training never ended. The long marches under extreme conditions, the war games in Louisiana, and the increase in new troops coming fresh out of boot camp gave me the assurance that war was soon to be. We were now in the late fall of 1941, and no Christmas furloughs were being issued nor were any long weekend passes given.

Again, we learned so much about how to endure cold and wet atmospheric conditions. One thing we were never allowed was umbrellas and other rain gear during rain and other types of falling weather. It was while on maneuvers and war games in Louisiana, during heavy midnight storms, after sleeping in pup tents, then awakening in the morning with water marks along our pant legs, we remembered our training so well. We would then move out before breakfast to engage an unseen enemy, travel all day and into the night, finally reaching a field kitchen with a lot of empty bellies then at last a beautiful ride back to Fort Sam Houston. Yes, that was how you learned to endure. It meant so much later on.

Another interesting experience that happened while serving at Fort Sam Houston was watching a parade of the most talented army units perform on the Division Parade Ground there. It was a beautiful sunny day, and the post band was playing. The flags were waving, and troops were marching in perfect rhythm. An old antique-looking tank was parked in front of the reviewing stand. After the review, the cover door to the tank opened and General George Patton stood and declared that there was not one soldier in the bunch! The tank door closed, and he went his merry way.

It was at this period in my service that an event occurred that meant little then but now is one of my fondest memories of my service at Fort Sam Houston. Such was the time Colonel Eisenhower came to Camp Bullis and taught our company how to build a tank trap. He was then assigned to the 2nd Infantry Division to ready it for future combat operations.

CHAPTER 4

Entry to the Air Force
and Training

It was December 7, 1941, when the news broke—Pearl Harbor had been attacked. A few days later, an alert was sounded at 2000 hours (8:00 p.m.). Two hours later, we departed Fort Sam Houston for destinations unknown to most of us. We traveled all night through wind and rain, arriving just at daybreak at an army installation on the Texas Gulf Coast. There, for the next sixty hours, we loaded supplies onto a waiting train, including field artillery pieces, 88 mm cannons, 105 mm cannons, and 37 mm cannons, large and small alike, anything that would propel a bullet. They were being shipped to the west coast to defend our cities, ports, and shores against what was then believed an imminent invasion by the Japanese forces that had laid waste to our pacific fleet the day before.

It was not long after that the sky was glistening with new and modern aircraft. The factories hummed night and day. The draft that filled the training camp and schools opened across the land to train our pilots and crews to man every ship and plane they built.

Thanks to those great leaders, and other men and women of wisdom and insight, they virtually had plans ready for such an expansion. The extent of such a rapid growth, although on paper, was great enough when needed to lead our country eventually becoming the "Arsenal of Democracy," supplying our allied partners under the Lend Lease Act. This really meant, "If you need it, we will bring it to you. You can pay for it later." Behind it all was, if we can't help you fight, we can furnish whatever you need.

Much has been said and much was written about our home front. Families were split up by the draft. Some were needed to move to factories and plants. Some were left to maintain the home and communities by working and planning life for those who went away to protect it.

New plans had to be made to cope with rationing and other shortages. Items like sugar, nylon, petroleum, etc., were in limited supply so you could only purchase them with a "ration stamp." People made victory gardens to provide their families food and many shared transportation, since the end of the automobile manufacturing for civilian use halted until the end of war.

All across our land life was far from easy. Many adults assumed responsibilities that they never had before. They helped in schools, driving school buses and filling in for teachers. They planned rallies to sell war bonds, which were augmented by soldiers on leave and dignitaries from Washington and others.

After our return from Palasios to our unit at Fort Sam, there was a notice on the bulletin board that anyone who wanted to become an aviation cadet and could meet the qualifications that accompanied the bulletin could do so. Several members of our company felt we met those requirements. Not long after this announcement, we were allowed to take the test. Only a few of us passed the written test and were directed to complete a physical examination. All of the ones who were chosen took the whole day test that included color-blind test, which almost disqualified several of us, but in the end, we did pass.

We were told to report back to our old units and we would be notified when and where we were to report. Several weeks passed when we were on training assignment at Camp Bullis that our orders came through for us to report to Brooks Field. There we were again, placed as they say on cold storage that lasted for weeks.

When we arrived, there was a fairly defined hurricane that had developed and struck as far in as San Antonio. We were called out to help during the high winds. The wind was blowing close to seventy miles per hour, toppling light planes on their back. I suggested that we roll out those jeeps and cars and trailers to tie them down.

The sergeant asked who said that.

I replied, "It don't make any difference, but let's go get them and talk later."

"I'm going to give you a blue ribbon," said the sergeant.

"Well, thanks," I said. Oh, anyway, it worked! I remember that General Eisenhower said after the war that the success of the Great Crusade depended on the many innovations by our American Troops.

Then came the orders for a new class to report to Kelly Field. So the end came for my friend McGrady and me to advance together. I was on the order, and he was sent to Falcon Field in Arizona. We never saw each other again for thirty-two years, long after the war.

Fast-forward through preflight school at Sad Sac Hill, a training center at Kelly Field. After completion of the training program, we were off on a daylong bus journey to our first stage of flight training, primary flight school, in Coleman, Texas. After three months of instructions by civilian barnstorming pilots, you can bet we were ready. We went through everything after we soloed, spins and stalls, slow rolls and loops, inverted spins, and then you were ready for final test by pilots from the Air Force.

We flew small open cockpit trainers that were powerful enough to train in aerobatics including stalls and spins as well as slow and snap rolls and loop with roll out. That was where the hint of trouble for me began. I felt a little pain during exercises where gravity and wind pressure on the body came into play. I had no trouble completing primary flight training, being the first of four under our instructor to solo. Then it was on to basic training. This was train-ing in larger planes with more powerful engines. All went well until again we started aerobatics. It became obvious that there was a problem when my maneuvers ended with blackouts while performing spin recoveries and complete loops. I had a choice of surgery to attempt a correction or to face elimination. I wanted to finish so badly that I chose surgery. Sadly, it did not work well enough, and because of time restraints, I was eliminated.

I was sent to an air base in Wichita Falls for recovery and to wait for radio operator class to begin at Scott Field, Illinois. Disappointed, you bet, but time and intense work in radio soothed the pain.

After months of study, building radios, studying antennas, receivers, transmitters, and hours and days of listening to Dot and Dashes, until it became a new language, we were finished, and from that ending forward, we were known as "static chasers."

Well, here we go. You would think we had been schooled enough and did everything but build an airplane. But no, we must now learn how to shoot one of them down. So off we go to Yuma, Arizona. There, we were taught how to field strip and even how to detail strip a pistol, a rifle, and a 50-caliber machine gun. But before I get ahead of myself, we first had to shoot down clay pigeons, a small ring made from clay. We did this to learn how to lead a target. After weeks of all this training, we flew under real conditions and fired at targets pulled by another plane.

Now we are ready to meet and form the crew that would go to war together. After a week leave at home, we met our pilot and crew in Lincoln, Nebraska. From Lincoln, we actually flew as a crew to Peyote, Texas, to begin our transitional training. Our stay at Peyote was cut short. We were transferred to Biggs Field in El Paso to make room in Peyote for B-29s, which required long runways and open country.

In transition, not much was learned by the crew. The training was directed to the pilot, the copilot, and the navigator. The remaining crew became rather bored on just formation. We had a few cross-country flights, some that kept us away overnight from our base.

Much like being awaken by a bad dream in the middle of the night, America was shaken and stunned by the double whammy attack on Pearl Harbor and the declaration of war that followed. A Japanese admiral said prophetically, "We might have awakened a sleeping giant." Oh, how true he was.

We saw the factories began to hum, and shipyards were filling the harbors. New planes, already designed, were dotting the training fields.

People began to realize how ill prepared this depression weakened nation was for the situation we were in. Our president summoned all military commanders and ordered all defensive measures be taken to meet the threat of a West Coast invasion. Sadly, but necessarily so, citizens of Japanese descent were placed in detention camps to prevent the possible consequences of fifth column activities in the event of the then expected invasion. At that point in time, our president and all military commanders, including General George C. Marshall, deemed this action absolutely necessary.

There were many who thought this was wrong and to be sure it was their right to do so. However, General George C. Marshall, whom President Roosevelt appointed as the able commander to prosecute the entire war, gave the final approval. Although time proved it was not necessary, it seemed that the decisions he made through the months and years of the war were the correct ones. Very few still remember how General Marshall planned and executed his program called The Marshall Plan, which helped the European nations recover from their war torn countries.

After pilot training, I find it more boring to describe training to be a radio man than training to be a pilot, so I will skip all the details, except to note we learned how to count dots and dashes, how to build a radio, and how to fire 50-caliber machine guns. Now we were ready to enter into training for our combat role as crewmembers.

As we entered this phase of our preparation for flying in combat, I remember that somewhere I saw hanging over the entrance to an airbase this sign, "Aviation itself is not inherently dangerous. But to an even greater degree than the sea, it is terribly unforgiving of any carelessness, incapacity, or neglect" (CPT A. G. Lampaugh). So to back that up, we made a pledge to make no mistakes.

CHAPTER 5

Deployment to Europe

The men who fly and fight their battles in the air have been called *flyboys*, *glamour nuts*, and *tender feet*. It began in the services of the prior century, and I'm sure it continues today. However, those who have tested the waters of the high-altitude training, subfreezing temperatures, oxygen breathing, and frostbite had a different take. Some even wrote, "What fools those mortals be?" (Shakespeare). The real experience in aviation is quite different than that portrayed in the movie series *Twelve O'Clock High* which incidentally was written and developed by our former group commander, Colonel Bernie Lay. Colonel Lay led one of the first missions our group flew and was shot down over France. He came out through the French underground and for fear of exposure of the recovery system of our downed airmen and others was not allowed to fly in that theater again.

Flying combat was not only a physical challenge but also a terrible mental challenge. Some of the equally harrowing experiences came before our combat began. Once on a formation training mission out of Biggs Airfield in El Paso, the old model B-17 started losing altitude. It was out of fuel. Immediately, we dropped out of formation and started transferring what fuel we had left to the two middle engines. Luckily, we were not so far away from the field, but we had a mountain to clear. We were forced to follow the old mathematical axiom that the shortest distance between two points is a straight line. The problem was we had a mountain in the way. Maintaining level flight caused one of the two engines to fail, since the gravity flow fuel tanks caused the dead engine to restart when losing altitude or going nose down. Again, we were faced with a problem. Did we have enough altitude to clear the mountain?

Strained voices and tense moments finally gave way to seeing the mountain hundreds of feet below us and the city of El Paso in sight. Although we had the mountain out of the way, we were still faced with having to lose altitude to keep both engines running as we reached the last part of our journey. Perhaps a bit of levity would help now. Someone said, "Maybe if need be, we could now glide further with four empty gas tanks!"

Guess what happened. As the nose became lower on our approach, all four engines, including the two that had been wind milling (feathered), started up—another ghost here.

Again, for unknown reasons, our crew was chosen as part of a group to fly our plane to Europe by the northern route through Iceland. Normally, women through the southern route crossing the warm southern Atlantic Ocean flew the replacement planes.

We began our journey, and it was a journey, by departing an airbase in Nebraska, to New Hampshire, on to Labrador, landing at a field in Goose Bay. The flight from Goose Bay required, among other considerations, that the weather conditions in Iceland at our time of arrival were perfectly calculated because in winter the nights were so short. We would depart Goose at sundown to arrive in Iceland at sunup. It was a six-and-a-half-hour trip. Days and days passed before the weather allowed our first departure. Finally, the snowplows cleared the runway, and as the sun began to set, we took off with the bomb bay full of bags of GI mail. Some three hours later, off the coast of Greenland, we received the message to return to Goose Bay due to the weather. I remember telling the pilots, "If you need me wake me up, I'm on the floor asleep."

A few more days at Goose, we were told to prepare to leave that night. The departure was again at sundown for the flight. Even the newly built and new model bombers would vary in fuel consumption, especially when loaded, as we were, with some five thousand pounds of mail bags along with our personal belongings and full fuel tanks.

Everything went well until the early morning hours when we knew we would not and could not be called back to Goose for we had crossed the point of no return. Time passed slowly, and our pilot became anxious, and often he called the navigator for reassurance we were on course. Again, time and distance became a deep concern. More often it was shown by another call to the navigator as a double check of location. The fuel also became a concern. The pilot's voice became more tense and occasionally wavering. I did call him and tell him that the radio traffic was increasing and becoming louder. He was pleased. It was still rather dark, but dawn began breaking as we received a call from the tower that we were cleared to enter traffic. Tired and hungry but happy, we touched down on a rather short runway. When we made our turnaround at the end of the runway, water from the ocean was splashing upon our wing.

After we had completed our long overwater flight from Goose Bay in Labrador to Iceland, I began to realize that we were among the limited few, if not the only crew, to make that flight in complete darkness with what we now know was the crudest method of navigating overwater. This was especially important after a previous attempt that had to be recalled because of bad weather in Reykjavik, Iceland. I can then and now understand the anxiety of our pilot toward the last few lingering moments of our flights. Well, we all recovered from that after several hours of sleep and great treatment by the locals.

Then we made the last two-hour leg of our journey in beautiful sunny weather, landing in Stone, England, the point of entry to the United Kingdom. A couple of days rest, it was on to our base and the beginning of our combat preparation that began a month later. I have mentioned how well we were treated a time or two. I want to add that at every emergency, when we were forced to land, we were treated equally as well.

During our pre-combat time, we became acquainted with some veterans that showed us a lot of things they had learned on the missions they had flown. They taught us how to use our flack jackets and to keep our parachutes in a safe and familiar place so if the time came and we were to use them, we would not have to waste time finding them. They also taught us other things we might be confronted with, such as repairing control cables that could be damaged or broken by flack or gunfire. They showed us this and a lot of other things they had experienced during their combat flights.

Then it was on to Great Britain, it only took a couple of hours and once again receiving a great welcome. There, the reception crew was wonderful!

Being the port where most all military entered, it was exposed to the harassment by the Germans and their V-1 bombing. It was more of a distraction than destruction, as it made more noise than it did damage. The V-I was a jet-propelled pre-runner of the V-II, which was rocket-propelled. The V-I was a small aircraft-looking apparatus that flew much like a plane and was powered by a grain alcohol motor that puff-puffed along. It was supposed to run out of fuel when it reached the target at Stone. The local ground crew told us that when the thing would crash, they would all run after it, turn it over, and drain the remaining alcohol out. Then they would pour it through light bread and have an Adolf Cocktail after five o'clock.

"Crockett's Crew," Happy Warriors
(From L to R, top row) Jerry Redlin, waist gunner; Jack
O'Toole, engineer; Ralph Graham, radio operator; Ed
Stamper, tail gunner; Rod Ludtke, lower ball turret;
Tommy Slaughter, bombardier; Paul Crockett, pilot;
Maynard Smith, copilot; and Bob Mills, navigator

CHAPTER 6

The Beginning of the
End in Europe

On December 24, 1944, the largest air attack of WWII was carried out when more than three thousand planes were dispatched against the German forces during the Belgium Bulge Counter Offenses. Perhaps to many, this mission seemed like just another day's work during this period, other than the number of planes in the one air battle. The sixty ME-109 German fighter planes attacked the one squadron that led the heavy bombardment stream toward the German target.

Normally, there would be a heavy dread to tackle another day in war, but this day was different. Everyone was eager and ready to go. While briefing for the mission that morning, we were again reminded as to how desperate the situation was on the ground for the allied troops and how they were looking for support. We were instructed to enter below twenty thousand feet so troops on the ground could not only see help coming but also hear the roar of the engines to boost their morale.

The following is an account of the event that occurred on Christmas Eve 1944. As purported, a young German scientist discovered an unusual weather phenomenon developing out over the North Sea. This weather condition was rare, but it had happened before in Northern Europe resulting in extremely heavy fog that covered the entire continent. This discovery was passed on to the German high command resulting in readying a counteroffensive against the Allied Forces who would be approaching from the west. Knowing their forces would be immune from the Allied Air Forces which were grounded across the channel in Great Britain, the German commanders launched their panzer divisions as well as streams of ground personnel as the fog moved in.

For eight days and nights, the fog was so dense that even in England the delivery trucks on the base had to be escorted by flashlights. The surprised Allied Forces retreated under heavy fire and troop movement. The following days, the report was the same as our forces continued to pull back. Day after day, the news continued badly, as we in the grounded Air Forces sat helpless listening to the report. Losses were such that many Air Force personnel were sent to the front for support. One week passed. Then, finally, at midnight of December 23, the fog lifted as suddenly as it came. Awakened in the early morning by noises of planes, engines warming and testing, trucks moving, and teletypes chattering, we knew what was happening. Up in the sky, the stars looked like polished diamonds. All across the British Isles, activities were the same, preparing for a maximum effort.

When it became time to go, we proceeded being led by a young brigadier general named Fred Castle. Under his command, he led the entire 8th Air Force toward the targets. As our crew approached the runway and prepared for takeoff, because of electrical failure, the cockpit determined through thorough and extensive tests that our plane was not air worthy preventing our turn to go. We returned to the flight lines to switch planes. Some 12 minutes were required to transfer parachutes, flack vests, logs, etc., that threw us behind some forty miles. Some time passed until a message came that our squadron was under attack. Being alone, we were told by General Castle to join another squadron.

After we received the notice that our squadron was under attack and was told to join another group, we proceeded to find a new group of warriors that would accept us. We had heard that odd planes or even odd wings (three plane groups) were not all that easy to do. First of all, you had to identify your situation on giving acceptable reasons on why you wanted to join. You had to give proper identification and the daily password that was a word that was common throughout such as Yankee Stadium or Grand Canyon, one that was readily recognized. Finally, after we were accepted, we really needed to know where we were going and what our mission was. We were told that our mission was to destroy a long steel girder bridge over a wide river and were told to drop at the same time as the lead aircraft.

The reason a squadron was so reluctant to accept an odd airplane was, the Germans had a history of patching up old planes that had been shot down and then filling them with machine guns, coming up and entering a group through fake identification, or falling in behind and hiding in the contrails the bombers were creating.

You have to remember we were bombing bridges and other targets that just a few days before were in territory we had occupied but had surrendered during the counter-offensive. Anyway, we were at a very low altitude, and after the drop, we could easily see the results. We could not see the results of our own drop but could see the bridge lying in the water as we gathered at our rally point for the flight back home.

It seemed such a waste to destroy that long expensive bridge, but of course, it was to prevent the rapid retreating German armies from its use as they tried to escape the trap the advancing Allied Armies had set.

It was after we had returned from the mission that we learned that our squadron and it alone had been hit by some sixty ME-109 fighter planes. The entire squadron, thirteen planes (actually just twelve without us), had engaged in battle. Our P-51 fighter escort had been delayed as they were stationed at the only place on the continent where the fog had not lifted. It was reported that five consecutive waves of twelve German fighters had attacked. Nine planes knocked out, either crashed or forced landed in Belgium. Thirty-four men died including General Castle who ordered his crew to bail out. He was to attempt to guide his crippled plane safely away from troops on the ground since being over friendly territory. Instead however they shot him down.

Brigadier General Frederick Walker Castle, CMH
Portrait hanging in Castle Air Museum, Atwater, California

When we returned to our base and our pilot walked into 836th squadron headquarters, our SQD commander who did not fly this mission exclaimed, "Man, I'm looking at a ghost." He had been informed that our crew along with eight others had been shot down or emergency landed in Belgium.

The facts referred to in the proceeding passages as to where we were and how close it happened prevented our ability to make the officials understand. Primarily because during the time between when we were to take off and returned to change aircraft, no one ever missed us, and no one in the squadron realized there was only twelve planes involved in the air battle. The records were never corrected.

HISTORY OF THE 487TH BOMBARDMENT GROUP
FOR DECEMBER 1944

Adverse weather again prevailed in December calling for the almost exclusive use of instrument bombing. Special navigational and bombing techniques were studied.

Eleven of the briefed missions became operational over enemy territory in December. Toward the end of the month, weather permitted more missions to be flown, some of which were visual. Considering the numerous night take-offs and poor visibility conditions, the 478th Bombardment attained an excellent record having had no accidents.

December will long be remembered by the men then assigned, however, by the truly historic mission of 24 December 1944.

For more than a week, the German counter-offensive in the Ardennes, aided by an impenetrable blanket of fog which grounded Allied aircraft, had been reaching out towards Liece and the Meuse River. The situation of the American First Army was admittedly serious. When the day before Christmas dawned bright and clear, the Eighth Air Force dispatched the greatest aerial armada seen to date in this or any other war. Over two thousand bombers and nearly one thousand fighters composed this mighty force.

When at last the huge air fleet turned back towards its bases in England, German Supply depots and communications systems feeding the German offensive lay shattered. For the 487th Bombardment Group there had been outstanding achievements. The leadership of this greatest aerial armada of all time was allotted to the 487th Bombardment Group. The command of the mission devolved upon Captain Mayfield R. Shilling when the aircraft bearing the original leader, Brigadier General Frederick W. Castle was shot down. The Group suffered its first major attack by enemy fighters.

In grim anticipation of a giant Allied aerial offensive with the return of good weather, the enemy mustered all available fighters to thwart this attack, which, if successful, would paralyze their attacking ground forces. It was inevitable that they should single out the lead aircraft for special attention. Thus some 50 enemy fighters joined in deadly combat with our bombers. Nine of our bombers never returned from this mission. Despite this staggering loss, the 487th Bombardment Group accounted for thirteen enemy fighters destroyed and several others damaged or probably destroyed. Nor was the 487th Bomb Group deterred from the fulfillment of its mission.

Although all our aircraft did not return, 43 aircraft from the First Bombardment Division diverted to our base on completion of this epoch mission, weather conditions over their home bases forbidding a landing. All available personnel devoted their Christmas Eve to the accommodation of the diverted crews and the maintenance of the aircraft, all of which, almost without exception, had received some degree of battle damage. Clerks, whose muscles had long been dormant, helped load bombs. Others performed duties completely foreign to their assigned duties, for the great aerial offensive had to be kept rolling.

On the 14th of December Lt. Colonel Russell F. Fisher temporarily assumed the command of the 487th Bombardment Group in the absence of Colonel Robert Taylor, 3rd who was unable to fulfill duties due to severe illness.

On 28 December 1944 Colonel William K. Martin arrived and assumed command. Colonel Martin's enviable record made him a fitting commander to carry on and extend the notable record of this Group.

For their glorious record in the month of December, the men of the 487th Bombardment Group were commended, with great enthusiasm, by Gen. Arnold, Lieutenant General Spaatz, General Eisenhower, and Major General Partridge, Commanding General of the 3rd Air Division.

The 487th Bombardment Group was truly a veteran outfit now. Several enemy targets became very familiar to the combat crews as they returned to bomb them time and again, among them Mainz, Merseburg, Hannover, Kassel and Ludwigshafen.

He official report from our 487th Bombardment Group Flight Book, indicating the incorrect reporting of how many planes were shot down from our squadron.

We tried to make sense of what happened from the start. As a crew, we were at a loss to explain as to why a new airplane, just from the states, would not pass the testing and final checks at takeoff. After the events of that day, our crew would wonder and ponder and even look to the heavens for an answer.

When the original story and the account of that mission were written, the writer, whoever they were, was not aware of the missing plane which was ours. We were not involved in the air battle because of our take-off delay; therefore, that delay was what forced us to be so far behind that we were ordered to join another group. There were plenty of groups in the area that day, and we proceeded to do so. The twelve groups remaining in our original squadron were engaged in a battle with the attacking German ME-109 fighters. As the group we joined trailed behind them, our bombardier looked for signs of the battle and saw large and small fires on the ground. The final count was nine bombers and fourteen fighters down over friendly territory. It would be difficult to imagine how anyone under that kind of fire, when death and destruction ruled the moment, could come close to an accurate estimate. That observation in all likelihood came from higher in the squadron. The only report of missing crewmembers was gained by listing the ones that were not among the four planes that survived. Those planes joined the remaining squadrons and reported the missing in the nine planes that were shot down or forced to land near Liege Belgium. So out of the nine planes missing, one was ours who had joined another group. Some made a forced landing near Liege, and others crashed after being abandoned. Since we were over friendly territory during the attack, all of the survivors were picked up by our own troops on the ground.

Although our group (the 487th Bomb Group) received a presidential citation, the bravery and gallantry of those twelve crews were not then or ever sufficiently awarded. Throughout the fifteen to eighteen minutes of being assaulted by the German fighters, this formation, without a single fighter escort, fought back to knock out thirteen fighters shot down for sure, one probably, and two heavily damaged. I believe the record shows 33 dead out of 108 with some 24 survivors, it should have never happened that way. These are the facts. Just as we sat helpless across the channel in England, while the German Air Force and the entire European continent was covered in fog for eight days, our forces knew and their forces knew this day would come. For more than a week, their forces prepared as did ours. The big difference was when the big air battle began, the Germans were ready, and we were not. They had excessive air power, whereas we had not one fighter plane escort for the lead squadron. The only excuse was our escort was late. How could it happen when for eight foggy days and nights we failed to anticipate what we knew could possibly happen. The end results were that eight planes were lost in battle, four more crashed, thirty-three lives lost including Brigadier General Castle, and seventy-five brilliant flyers whose lives were forever changed.

Long after the war was over, our crew would have reunions at various cities, and we never failed to discuss that mission nor be thankful we were not involved in that tragic mistake. The air command never mentioned anything more than to say our fighter group was late nor did they ever change the number of planes lost from nine to eight.

It is not difficult to understand why in the end there was so much confusion and the mistakes the squadron suffered. The first and most costly mistake was the train of some two thousand bombers being sent to their target with the head group unescorted by the greatest fighting squadron ever. They could not make a rendezvous with the bomber group. Also, in order for the troops on the ground to see and hear the Air Force coming with help, we were flying at an altitude that's ideal for fighter groups to perform at top peak. This lower altitude spared the ME-109s the necessary time and fuel to climb to thirty thousand feet, which was the normal altitude for our bomb formation.

That alone is a relatively amazing accomplishment. It was only a short time later we realized what happened to our squadron. Just four planes returned that completed the mission. The crew that shared our Quonset hut for one night was missing. Even though we had known them for only one full day, we had gotten acquainted with them and had planned a Christmas party for that night. All our gifts lay on the lower cot up front. It was a very sad sight to behold. Instead of a party, we bagged up all the gifts a kid would want and sent them to a child's nursing home down in Lavenham and then came back and prepared for another mission Christmas Day. Memory doesn't serve me well enough to recall for sure whether we flew or not, but as the old saying goes, "When a horse throws you, the best thing to do to recover is to get right back up on the horse."

Don't try to imagine what it was like for a crew with largely eighteen- to twenty-four-year-olds that had completed only six missions to face such a bleak future. Only the training we received back in the states made it possible to continue.

A couple of days after the mission of our devastating loss, one of the crewmembers on one of the flights suffered a mental and emotional breakdown. It was said that breakdowns of this nature had occurred a few times before but not in such a devastating manner as those resulting from the battle of December 24. His problem was so bad he could not be treated there. He needed to be sent back to the states for treatment. Since Crockett, our pilot, was not involved in the attack, he was chosen to fly him to a Royal Canadian Air Force base in northern England where they had a plane that was leaving for the states the next morning. It then fell on the skeleton crew to fly with the pilot. The crew required a pilot, navigator, engineer, and radio operator. I recall stepping back in the waist to speak to him, but he was so sedated you couldn't communicate with him. He was dressed in civilian clothes to secure his rank and position. We always felt he might have been a copilot, since they are the only one on the plane that had nothing to do while under attack. The pilot of course was busy flying the plane, and everyone else had a gun position. I'm sure I could never imagine sitting for fifteen minutes watching planes disappearing around you and smoke and gunfire filling the air and sometime the plane losing parts. The ambulance was waiting when we landed. Every effort was made to aid his comfort and need.

Some shake-up of our command structure was required after one of the commanding officers of the Eighth Air Force visited our group. This resulted in reducing the number of aborted and take-off failures happening after the unprotected mission of December 24, 1944.

Also, our crew was reduced from ten to nine as many personnel were transferred to the short-handed ground forces. This created another duty and position for the radio operator as he moved to man one of the waist guns when under attack.

One of the greatest improvements that came out of the visits of the top command from the Eighth Air Force was the continuing fighter protection we received that carried us all the way to our target and back.

A lot of soul-searching began after the blood bath attack that occurred on Christmas Eve. Much more attention was given to fighter support for those slow-flying heavily loaded bombers as they delivered their assigned load and returned to their base. Extreme concern developed among the crew when on long missions, the fighter coverage became thin. Nevertheless, morale improved, and mission aborts began to decrease.

Out of the thirty-three missions my crew flew, this one mission contained so many losses, mistakes, failures, and mysteries that it was impossible to explain just what and how it happened in the six or seven hours it took to complete. One of the haunting questions we tried to understand was why in the official account of the mission the author of the report never mentioned that the group had no fighter support although hundreds of fighters were in the area and were available. There was no mention of the total loss of life but only to say nine planes were missing after the encounter.

History now reveals this as follows: just as the Russians on the eastern front allowed the German armies to create their own demise, so did the allies on the western front by employing the same tactics. As surprising and painful as it had to be, this destroyed Hitler's final hopes through the artful handling and managing of the Belgium Bulge counteroffensive operation. (The deep penetration that pushed us back so far because they knew the fog was coming and we didn't.)

The passage of time has dulled many of the more memorable events; however, some, if not all, of the accounts of this part of history are enshrined in General Castle's Museum near Castle Air Force Base in Merced, California. The museum was named in his honor after he was posthumously awarded the Congressional Medal of Honor.

This mission, as important and as effectively as it was, should be remembered as secondary to the effort of those brave forces on the ground that withstood eight dark days of hell called the Belgium Counteroffensive. For truly it was known then and recorded later as the beginning of the end of the war in Europe.

Finally, this account of that great moment in the history of WWII is important only if it sheds some light to those who were never fully aware of the Belgium Bulge Operation and how the gravity of the outcome so hastened the day of victory in Europe. For those of us who were a part of it, the memory will live forever, but more importantly, they will be remembered as the Greatest Generation.

Flight crew and ground crew

CHAPTER 7

Other Missions

The new beginning after an ill-fated Christmas, I remember writing a note to myself. Did I want to continue? It went something like this. "Did I have the guts to keep on going? Bye." As the radio operator back in the middle of the plane with the cabin heated room and the only crewmember with a swivel chair, naturally I was most hated and envied of the lot. However, they were Johnny-on-the-spot if I could offer something that sounded good with a little comfort. I first explained that we had to forget December 24 because we all knew it should not have happened if our group had had the fighter support and had we been flying at the normal altitude. Now, since fair weather returned, you can bet that we would have ample support from here on out. After a few more stump speeches, I became Uncle Ralph. They even offered me an orange from time to time. Of course, at 35,000 feet, the orange that they did give me was frozen and harder than the machine they were cleaning. So we all buckled down and flew one mission at a time, looking forward to the midway mark where we knew we would be going for a week of R&R (rest and recuperation).

As we continue our efforts to complete our tour of duty, we could not help to think of how lucky we have been so far. For me, Lady Luck has been a constant companion. Remember where it began. I began to think there was a correlation between the luck we were having and the ghostly event that seemed to regularly occur from time to time as we moved forward.

Everything seemed to go well for a while, and then there was trouble over Hamburg. We had reached our half-way point so R&R would be the next full week.

I should list close calls and the luck we had known and start counting missions one at a time. There were other missions that didn't go as planned. I recall the one to Hamburg to attack the submarine pens and docks. As we entered our bomb run, they covered our target with smoke. We had to do a 180-degree turn and redo the run again. This time, the target was clear, as the smoke had dissipated. Likewise, they had time to more closely determine our altitude, and the flack was heavy. As we left, a piece of flack struck the ammunition rack in the waist, and several rounds exploded knocking out the gunnery instructor. He normally would not have been there but was flying with us that day. I moved him to the radio room and covered him with a blanket. He then said he would be OK that he had not been hurt that bad.

Somewhere further along in this writing, I will make mention of our losses as a unit. We knew very early in the campaign that to defeat Germany and its air power, the source of fuel had to be eliminated. The Air Force had to do it. This meant the refineries not only in Germany but also others like the Romanian oil fields had to be attacked. We knew heavy loses would be endured. There would be not only huge material and weapons losses but also air-crews and planes.

From the beginning, aviation units and replacement crews coming in would have to be separated, so crews that trained together would not fly together so loses would not bear so heavily on surviving crews. This was just one of the indications of the hazards we faced.

It was during the invasions on D-Day that our group started its first loss with our group commander being shot down. He did survive and was picked up by the French underground, through their system of recovering aircrews and others. They helped him return in August.

One, in particular, was a mission to Berlin. The target was far past the city. I recall seeing the Berlin Olympic Stadium as we entered. At our altitude, it looked like a bent finger ring. Because of the Russian forces closing in on the Eastern front, most of their antiaircraft guns had been sent there and used as artillery pieces. After the bomb run and our drop had been completed, we began our return by dropping below ten thousand feet to get off of oxygen. Our mission commander had ordered this not realizing the antiaircraft command had placed guns on barges west of the city and had set a trap at ten thousand feet. We became sitting ducks. One of our flight crews took a direct hit that completely destroyed the nose of the plane, and the bombardier and navigator were lost with it. The time we had for observation was short, and we could not see and could not determine if there were any open chutes.

I don't remember that particular target, but the description of that event reminded me of another preparation on the flight line. We were briefed for a mission to Nuremberg to render the runways unusable but not destroy the airports.

We were ready to go at seven o'clock, and we waited and waited, and finally about nine o'clock, we received a red flair from the tower that meant the mission had been scrubbed. Patton had already taken Nuremberg. I don't recall which mission this was, but we didn't get credit for one.

I might add that more than once, in returning from a mission, our home base was weathered in, and it was necessary to fly north to find fair weather. Once, we landed at a RCAFB (Royal Canadian Air Force Base), and they were the greatest host. They opened the kitchen and fed us steaks with all the trimmings, then carried the ones who cared to go to a local pub out for the evening. For sure, I went.

The mission that carried us to the oil targets in Southeast Germany was the longest one we had flown. At the time we received the word, our base was closed due to weather. We were out of fuel. We were at only eight hundred feet, which was getting very close to bail out limits. The pilot told those who want to could bail out, as he would take it down alone if we chose to do so. I was asked what was I going to do. I said I would stay aboard in the event the pilot had trouble getting out of a forced landing. Everyone chose to do so as well, and we reached a field where the runway was open. Every effort was made by the high command to schedule flights all across Europe to meet with weather restraints. I do recall flying a weather mission one night and what they found that night was enough information to cancel the mission the following day.

But that was then, and we had more to do. We were flying several missions a week to finally close out by carrying leaflets on our final drop instead of bombs.

Someone once asked what we did during the days we didn't fly. There wasn't much to do on the base, but most of them were located near small towns and communities. We began to get really acquainted with the locals, and we questioned one another's likes and habits, which usually were very close to those at home. I once remember asking a fairly middle-aged lady what she thought of us Yankees. She said, "We were nice, but we were overpaid, overfed, oversexed and over here." We were often invited to join the local civilian employees who worked on base, to have tea with them about four o'clock. We would spend most of our time writing letters, sending and receiving mail, picking up our laundry, and going to the PX (post exchange). At first, we were kind of leery of that hot tea, but as time passed, you developed a taste and habit. We begin to look forward to that time of day.

Normally, on the weekend when we weren't scheduled to fly, we would go on pass to London and would spend our time at the USO as our headquarters. From there, you could go on tours of London that took us to sights of revolution, like the queen's palace, Westminster Abbey, and the Big Ben Tower. Our tour guide would point out those and other points of interest like the London Bridge, the Thames River, and the Changing of the Guard.

Nightlife included skating rinks and nightclubs and other interesting centers. Somewhere along the way, I met a young lady, and we dated several times. She invited me to spend the weekend at her home once. She really was a beautiful person and had a nice family. They lived probably ten miles from downtown London, and we rode the tram that carried us to within a couple hundred yards of their home.

The night I stayed there, she called out. "Mom, I brought a yank home."

Her mother yelled out, "He will have to sleep on the couch." They had a small house, and all the bedrooms were upstairs. I met them all the next morning, and they were very nice and friendly. After we talked a while, her father asked me if I happen to have an extra razor blade. I told him yes and handed him a new package of Gillett Blue blades. He was so elated that he called his wife saying, "Look what he gave me, enough to last till the war is over." He worked nearby, and I guess he was some kind of office employee. He left wearing a smile. He and her mom were so inter-ested in America. She inquired about where I was from and about my family. She wanted my home address, and later my mother received a letter from her. Her son wrote to my brother who was about the same age. It was an interesting exchange of letters. Later on, when I knew it would be my last date with her, she accompanied me to the train station. We both realized that this was the end for us. Although we never let our relationship become that serious, our departure was somewhat dramatic knowing that we would never be near again. We tried to keep it short with a little kiss on the cheek and a bye bye. There were tears, for we vowed that we would remember the good times, the fun, and the most intimate moments. We agreed they would be forever cherished.

The horror of war, the strain on our spirit, and the day-to-day repetition of the good, the bad, and the uncertainty of it all seem to demand that we have some good-natured manner and clean fun. I do remember one little episode while we were waiting in the aircraft for word to go. The pilot and a few others came back to the radio room. The pilot stood there in playful shock and awe exclaiming what a beautiful compartment I had and asked if I was going to get some curtains. I replied that I eventually was, but I wanted to get me a recliner first. A couple of the other pokes chimed in telling the pilot they would help load it through the bomb bay. Before I told them to leave, I described the pilot's seat. It reminded me of the old horse-drawn wiggle-tail riding cultivators that I used on the farm that had lines, leavers, and peddles. I used it long enough to learn how to fly a plane and didn't know it. About that time, we received a green flare from the control tower, meaning prepare for takeoff. The fun ended, the escape hatch closed and latched, and from now on, it was strictly business.

Special recognition is due to the great people of Belgium for all the inconveniences and suffering as the continued accordion-type movement of the conflicting armies crisscrossed back and forth across their country. First, it was the

Germans moving in, then the American invasion pushing them back, then the Belgium Bulge Operation driving the allies almost to the sea, and finally the Belgium Counter Offense for the final drive across their land to end the war. This was in addition of course to the bombing by the Allied Forces. During the first part of the war after the invasion, both Brussels and especially Liege were bombarded twice in the month of May 1944.

Remembering that we had bombed Liege earlier and how nice they were in helping recover the wounded the day of the air battle reminded me of the old bar-room adage: that the toes you step on are not all that far from the ass you may someday have to kiss.

Following these massive strikes, the Air Force in Europe increased steadily sometime up to four or five missions in a row. Just as it did in all crews, the strain of combat began to take its toll. Some showed little signs of flack happiness; this was when a member would laugh at things that weren't funny. So about February 1, we were told we would be going to spend a week on rest and recreation.

On the first day, we were bused to a place called Walhampton House in Southern England. While there, for seven days, we lived like the king for which this place was designed and built. Everything we desired was there or made available for us. We climbed trees, shot bow and arrows, and played games. We also went on tours and met some really great people. The restfulness was really helpful. We were exhausted! The days passed rapidly, and it soon was time to return for the rest of our work.

Walhampton House, Southern England
Primary R&R location

Relaxing in the woods near Walhampton House

As we began the remainder of our tour, we could tell our missions had become somewhat easier although we did lose some because of our mistakes.

It was a beautiful clear day, and everything went well on our takeoff run and the climb to altitude. We had been over the English Channel for a short time when I noticed through my small window near the 1 and 2 engines something that I thought was vapor crossing the wing. After a few seconds, I looked back through the window, and the vapor had changed to smoke. I immediately called the pilot and reported what I saw. Soon, he and the engineer were busy attempting to feather the prop. For several minutes, their attempt was failing. The pilot told me to get everyone back in the waste of the plane and get ready in the event we had to abandon ship. He said be sure that they put on their Mae West (their water life vests) on first and then their chute harness.

It was touch and go for the next few minutes before they finally got the engine feathered and everything settled down. Since we were in the channel, it was not far from the designated spot to drop the bombs. They were still pinned and would never explode. I can't recall for sure, but I believe this was the only incomplete mission that we flew. We never liked to lose an engine, but that had happened a time or two when they would overheat or get hit by flack and then have to be shut down.

All down through the thirty-three missions that our crew flew, we were asked to be aware of anything that was different on each one. Having flown the entire tour in the winter months, there were problems that you didn't encounter in warm weather. The temperature at high altitude varied with the temperature on the ground. As a general rule, it decreases two degrees every one thousand feet. So at the altitude we flew, the temperature would sometime reach forty degrees below zero. This required heated suits, flight jackets, and scarves to prevent frostbite. Many times, as you exhaled your warm breath air, it would freeze up in the flutter valve of your oxygen mask. You would have to break it up with your hand in order to exhale.

Our tail gunner was a nineteen-year-old kid, and as I have said before, our worst enemy was the three F's—flak, fighters, and frostbite. I remember so well when he would crawl out over and around the tail wheel, cables, and oxygen supply lines how he looked. His eyebrows were covered with his frozen breath and ears red with frostbite. Although he wore an electrically heated suit, it was the loneliest and the coldest place on the plane. Fortunately, there were not too many missions due to a short winter where the temperature was forty to sixty degrees below zero.

After the terrible loss on Christmas Eve 1944, there were some that were bad, and some were what we called milk runs.

Our missions were completed on March 19, 1945, when we flew our last. Although it was early spring, it still seemed odd to have a beautiful day in England. This was our final mission, and no one was mentioning it for fear it would jinx us. This was, of course, our final takeoff, and we were all kind of tensed up until we had a lift off and started climbing. Then we noticed how quickly we became airborne and now realizing we were carrying leaflets instead of our regular load. That gave us a much better and loftier feeling. Our mission was the marshaling yards or the rail center in the city of Leipzig. Leipzig was on the border of East Germany and the smaller countries like the Czech Republic and Poland. Everything went well until we had almost reached the IP, the point where we began our bomb run. Suddenly, it was decided that we were abandoning our primary target and switch to either our secondary target or finally a target of opportunity. Abandoning our primary target was probably because of endangering the masses of refugees flowing into the West ahead of the advancing Russian armies.

Zwickau was our final target. Only a few, which didn't include us, knew immediately what or when the drop would occur. Just as we reached the bomb run, the flack began to fill the air ahead. The bomb run for a load of leaflets seemed to last forever. There were no fighters for us on our final sweat. The flack attacks seemed to black out the sun. Finally, a clearing came, and it was a relatively short distance by air, but it seemed to take forever to reach and clear the target.

We looked back at the thousands of leaflets flowing down behind us. We would soon cross the Rhine and be headed home to England.

Whether it was the relief or just because it was all over, or the feeling of accomplishment of doing something that few ever did, we all agreed, some with tears in their eyes and others weeping openly, that somewhere out there was a guiding hand that was with us to the finish.

On the last leg of our flight and our final landing, it was a plain and simple mass celebration. There were all types of banter among our crew. As the radio operator, I was the butt of the jokes. Some dove hunter that they drafted to cover one of the waste guns yelled out, "Can you celebrate with international Morse code up there?"

I replied, "I don't have any dots and dashes left. I used them all up making sure we got your ass back to safety in bad weather." It went on and on until the pilot did a cake-walk down the runway to meet a fabulous ground crew who joined our celebration.

Thankful, humble and lucky, the tri-factor gave us the grand feeling of accomplishments in the work we were each assigned to do on the missions we flew. The end was great, and only a few more days we were headed home.

Not many WWII vets are still around, and fewer of us remain who were there and ready when Pearl Harbor was attacked. Few remember President Roosevelt speaking on an old Philco radio, with a weak vacuum tube causing his voice to rise and fall, asking congress to declare war and believing with God's blessing we would gain an inevitable triumph.

Some of those dark days have faded, and some never will, for a lot of time has passed and things are different. The world has changed. One man goes to war, and another one returns. I still get goose bumps when I hear those six words in our national anthem, "That our flag was *still* there."

CHAPTER 8

Discharge and
Homeward Bound

I remember the sacrifices our people at home had to make and the sacrifices the people in the war zones had to make as well but to a much greater degree. One of the things that impressed me the most was the streets and buildings destroyed by the German Air Force blitz. Yet the people pressed on.

On one of the tours of London, there were already buildings that were either totally or partially destroyed. Very seldom was the rubble removed from the streets. You might wonder how the German Air Force could be that accurate when bombing at night while it was completely blacked out. Being in radio work, I understand a little bit about how they could cross two radio signals over the target and they would signal the bomb release. The British, however, got wise to that and from a submarine out in the channel used the same technique and crossed the signals short of the target. They landed in a sugar beet field twelve miles short! You can bet the British RAF (Royal Air Force) were waiting.

Prime Minister Winston Churchill, the great British Empire leader and a wonderful fan of the RAF, made many quotes regarding their success. One was on a cigarette package holder that to this day I jealously guard. It said, "Never in the field of human conflict was so much owed by many to so few." He also commented. "The gratitude of every home in our Island, in our Empire, and indeed throughout the world, except in the abodes of the guilty, goes out to the British airmen who, undaunted by odds, unwearied in their constant challenge and mortal danger, are turning the tide of the World War by their prowess and by their devotion." Again, I try to steer clear of politics, but when you see great leaders like Churchill as well as President Bush (41) denied reelection, you just have to stand aside while the hairs on the back of your neck lay back down.

Shortly after completing our tour of missions, a request came to our group for radio operators. One of the calls was from a station not far from ours. I never knew for sure why, but I was transferred to fly with instructors training replacement crews for combat. It took only a couple of flights until I decided to go to the flight surgeon and complain since I had already completed my tour. He asked me about my combat record, and I told him I had finished my tour. He told me to go to my room and not to report to fly again and that a jeep would pick me up the next morning and carry me and my records to Stone, the port where we would leave to return home. There, I crossed paths with some of my old crew, but I was arriving, and they were moving then to board a ship, so we didn't get to talk long.

Now the great conflict was over in Western Europe. The people were rejoicing throughout the land. Hitler and Mussolini were gone, and the people were free. The old bombers were parked against the fences and most probably will be sold for scrap.

We were headed home on an old Spanish excursion boat of the British Company in charge of transporting troops back across the ocean to the United States and Canada. The old pleasure ship had a swimming pool in the middle, and it really squeaked when the waves hit it. It only made nine knots, but a bullhorn from the other ships in the convoy blared out, "We must speed up or we would be on our own."

We are in the middle of the Atlantic Ocean homeward bound, and we just learned the Armistice Papers had been signed. The convoy was churning through stormy waters fighting swells ten to twenty feet high.

Not much less disturbing and unsettling was my own personal situation of having to cope with decisions of the five years having been made by the government. First, I had to decide whether to continue my service career or accept a discharge. The decision was solely up to me. The war in the Pacific was still raging, and we have no clue or hint of a quick ending of hostilities. To accept a discharge through the points system and to return to civilian life seemed more desirable. I knew for some of us the decision was simple. Many anxiously returned to civilian life and assumed their old jobs which awaited them back home. To those like myself, who grew into manhood in an army home, the outlook was a little different. After a lot of soul-searching, my final decision was to return home and begin a new career. After a few days at home and getting adjusted to a more civil way of living, I decided a little vacation time might be in order before deciding what to do with my life.

During an interview once, someone asked if the overall combat experience affected my life after the war was over. My answer was, "It could and certainly would have if I let it." At first, it required a lot of self-examination. I tried to maintain a close relationship with my family and friends asking them to bear with me as I again resume civilian life. Knowing it was such a trying experience going from the strains of war to the quiet and loneliness, I had to decide how to start making plans on my own. I knew it was necessary for me to recognize and appreciate those things I learned and how to apply them in civilian life. Having been away so long because of the war, I was denied the first couple of rungs on the ladder we climbed to attain the great American dream.

I did, however, take advantage of the GI Bill and got a couple of years of JR College work on a work-study basis. Among the subjects I chose, the two I believe helped me the most was a course I took in Bible study, and the other was English literature. I always thought it helped me in communicating my thoughts. Just to finish let me explain I never captured much of the dream but was far from unsuccessful. I finished the courses with one of the greatest families ever, and they truly do overwhelm me with pride every day I live.

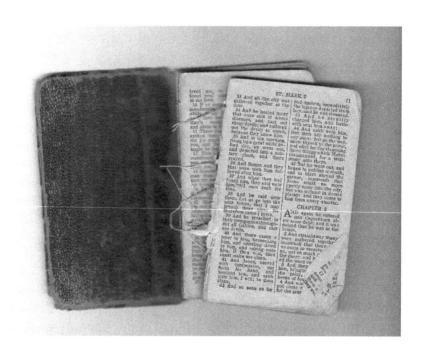

"Old Standby"
Pocket Bible I carried on every mission

CHAPTER 9

Reunions

Our crewmembers began several reunions. After forty-four years had passed since we had been together, it was one day in 1989 that I look at my telephone and with some trepidation gathered enough courage to pick it up and call a number that my tail gunner gave me before we parted in England. The phone rang one time, and a lady answered, and truly it was Ed's wife. To my delight, she was about as excited as I was when I explained who I was. We had a very interesting talk. Ed was at a meeting, and she would have him call as soon as he returned. Not only did he call, but his daughter also called. She was equally excited. So from there on with everyone's help, our crew was located, and a series of reunions began.

From the first meeting on, it seemed that the mission of December 24, 1944, became one of the topics of discussion. We all were thinking of how fortunate we were and long wondered what happened to the new plane we had to turn back that took the twelve minutes which might have saved our lives. Had we been on the initial flight, we surely would have had much more to recover from.

During the entire time of our tour in combat missions, our crew often talked about the lack of association with the other crews in our group. The Quonset huts, where we lived, were scattered fairly well across the base, and about the only time we saw and talked to members of other crews was at breakfast before each mission, with exception of course the crew in our own hut.

It was many years after the war, while trying to find members of our crew in order to have a reunion, we learned some of the reasons we were kept apart. Early in the aviation history, the losses were so heavy that the morale dipped very low among our surviving crews and the percentage of missions completed was also low as it was too painful to discuss. The overall losses from beginning until finish varied from 48 to 52 percent. In the earlier missions, the losses, of course, were much heavier because of the length of the missions and the lack of fighter plane support. The missions our crew flew were later and had established fighter support bases well inside the continent and could support us all the way to the target. The mission on our Christmas attack and the losses suffered that day raised the loss percentage for our squadron to 73 percent.

Our crew, remembering how shocked we were, began to realize that our loses shouldn't have been and wouldn't have been if we had had our fighter escort. However, we still felt the pains of losing the lives of so many due to lack of preparation for the attack.

During reunions, we often talked about the strange and ghostly things that happened during our tour as well as in our training back home. So haunted by every seemingly close call and near miss, we named the story of the mission of December 24 The Ghost of the Counteroffensive Attack During the Belgium Bulge Offensive. To a man, we agreed perhaps it wasn't all luck. We unashamedly declared, as stated before, that somewhere among the celestial landscape, there was a guiding hand that led a bunch of kids through that valley of the unknown.

First crew reunion, 1989

Reunion 1989. Crew and wives

Several times, our crew would gather at various locations. One of those was in California where we made a side trip down to Merced and visited General Castle's Museum that was opened after the Castle Air Base that was named in his honor was closed. The museum was full of Air Force pictures and memorabilia including actual B-17 cutaways and many other things relative to the general's service and flight history. What was lacking was information about the mission that he flew and the accounts surrounding the attack that caused him and so many more their final sacrifice.

The only thing they had was a picture of his crashed aircraft on the ground. I inquired about who and how many of the crews that survived that day had visited the museum. The manager said no one except a few of his nieces and nephews had been there. After which I realized he had nothing about the mission other than the date and that it happened in Belgium and a picture of the remains of his plane.

They were skeptical at first about our being on the mission and were weary of the information I was giving them until I presented them a copy of the letter which I wrote explaining the history of the eight days we could not fly. I gave them a copy of that letter and a picture of our crew, and he hung it under the picture of General Castle.

The more I thought about why there were no more visitors, I began to realize again how few on that mission had an opportunity to know what happened so quickly. It was long after that day it began to occur to me that so few had a chance to remember. I thought, *Sure, my crew and I were so far away from it and actually couldn't have known until it was all over.*

We were happy to provide so much information including the letter and the picture. After they began to know we were for real, we were detained and really made welcome as they showed their appreciation of our visit.

After we had completed most of our reunions, it seemed that everyone was interested in writing a book or wanted to have one written. We all agreed that if anyone would start a book, all the rest of us would contribute as much as we could to help him. Time passed, and one by one they began to pass away. Finally, on the last of our reunions, there were only three of us left. Today, as I attempt to finish this account of one of the most infamous combat encounters, I, the writer, am the only surviving member of our crew.

2016 Air Show in Waco, Texas
Ralph Graham stands in front of B-17 prior
to boarding the plane for a flyby

CHAPTER 10

If Not for Those Twelve Minutes

Before I finish, I feel I must, on behalf of our entire crew, mention some of the things that bothered us the most. Walking into our quarters and seeing the five empty bunks with Christmas gifts they had received from home; we had planned a Christmas party that night. Also, we knew we would have to mail their personal belongings soon. In that very spot, that young kid not over eighteen or nineteen years old personally asked, "How do I adjust the control on my heated suit?"

Now my final thoughts will be about myself. Happiness is real when you dream of home and with a lot of God's blessings you step upon the porch and open this door, hence that great feeling after going so far away. Anyway, I made it after so many times I didn't really believe it would happen. It was made easier by picking up that do-it-yourself kit that our maker told us to do in his book.

Back home now, I spent a lot of useless time until I met the love of my life that became my wife on April 20, 1946. We became very proud parents of a great balanced family of two boys and two girls. Everyone knew how proud we were of them, and they managed their lives beautifully through the years. We have always been a very close family, but on September 13, 1997, our lives were crushed when God took our mother and wife suddenly. We never knew the cause, but she collapsed after eating lunch. She never suffered but went in peace. Our family yearned for a lot of things we might not have, but love was not among them.

A happy moment with my loving wife, Nell Graham

My children have their own families, and no one could ever ask for a better group. Out of these four families, there are ten grandchildren, twenty-six great grandchildren, and eleven great-great grandchildren. Recently, I attended our annual family reunion and what a beautiful sight it was. Some were playing ball, some were fishing, and many were singing, eating, and laughing. I stood in mortal silence, and somewhere behind them was a wide opening, with the sun shining through. I wondered in awe what that scene would have looked like if not for those twelve minutes when we waited to change planes on our sixth mission December 24, 1944.

As the sun faded away, so must the story of a grateful soul who volunteered to serve his country for one year but completed fifty-five months until our work in Europe had ended, filled with moments of horror, some grief, and emotional trauma, yet blessed to have found strength in a wonderful crew.

The End

The memories linger on and will be passed down to all of my descendants. This is me with my family, celebrating Christmas 2019. It's amazing what a twelve-minute delay can result in, and twenty-two were unable to attend!

ACKNOWLEDGMENT

The year was 1910, and William Howard Taft was president. The US population was ninety-two million. The national debt was $1.15 million. Telephones and traffic lights were invented. Federal spending was just one-half billion. Popular toys were erector sets, tinker toys, and the Ouija board. Yes, it was 1910 that the United States was first mentioned as a world power. The gathering clouds of unrest and uncertainty began in Europe as the dreadful prospects of WWI began to surface. These and other events reflect the tone and tenor of the times when young folks were planning their future. A young man with an unexpected turn of good fortune was able to purchase the one, if not the only, Peter Shetland Buggy in his community. That was enough to draw the attention of all the young ladies and a special okay from the one among them that he had long since known would be his own. After she accepted his proposal in marriage, the legacy of Ed and Mamie's life began. Like so many families, young and old alike, they were caught up in the turmoil of the westward movement. Families with their belongings were moving in the turn of the century expansion to seek a better life. Ed and Mamie too were on the move, renting and sharing homes with friends in order to make ends meet while saving to buy a home of their own.

It was the year 1925 when they purchased their new home where they spent the rest of their life with the exception of a two-year stint in an adjoining county where they met and made lifelong friends. The land they bought was raw and new and offered rich rewards through farming and ranching; however, it required hard work and a persistent effort. Trees and underbrush had to be cleared. Tanks for the livestock had to be dug, and fences had to be built. It was through this endeavor they together taught us as a family and showed us by example the strength and pioneering spirit to accomplish what they did. Along the way, we watched as we worked and learned as we listened how the real lesson of one's character became so pronounced, so profound, and so important.

Let me finish by saying Mom and Dad never set a stern set of rules and demands for us to follow. Rather they did by example to live the lifestyle found in that great Book of Life they were taught to follow. It has been one hundred years since that union, and each year almost without fail our families have gathered to remember. The lives they lived were not complicated but far from simple. It left such an indelible mark we dare not forget.

My parents, Ed and Mamie Graham

ABOUT THE AUTHOR

Ralph Graham came from a large family in the farming community of Athens, Texas and learned the true value of family living through the Great Depression years. After graduating from high school in 1940, he and his lifelong friend decided to enlist and serve their country verses continuing with their first job. At eighteen years of age he was the  youngest member of his company, war was not a consideration at the time. Nothing could have prepared him for what he would experience as the United States declared War after the bombing of Pearl Harbor December 7, 1941. He soon developed skills he did not know he processed. Taking responsibilities and leadership were a few of those characteristics he developed. As combat was inevitable, he became recognized by his peers and crew as the steady leader who kept the rest of his crew calm and always giving words of encouragement in most difficult situations. After his service years he was an entrepreneur and became not only a home builder but an inventor always using his mind. He recently celebrated his ninety-eight birthday on April 9, 2020 with family and friends who paid their respect to one of the last members of the Greatest Generation. Today he still swings the golf club, drives himself to the course, and collects winnings by regularly placing in the top three. His life lessons are among the most valued blessings to those who can spend time because of that one fateful day in 1944 when God decided to keep his crew around for even more important things.

CPSIA information can be obtained
at www.ICGtesting.com
Printed in the USA
LVHW111003161020
668988LV00007B/171